Write a

Romance

in 5 Simple Steps

Creative Writing in 5 Simple Steps

Suzanne Lieurance

Enslow Publishers, Inc.
40 Industrial Road
Box 398
Berkeley Heights, NJ 07922
USA
http://www.enslow.com

Library of Congress Cataloging-in-Publication Data

Lieurance, Suzanne.
Write a romance in 5 simple steps / Suzanne Lieurance.
p. cm. — (Creative writing in 5 simple steps)
Summary: "Divides the creative writing process into five steps, from inspiration to publishable story, and includes in-depth treatment of the romance genre with writing prompts"—Provided by publisher.
Includes bibliographical references and index.
Includes webliography.
ISBN 978-0-7660-3837-0
1. Love stories—Authorship—Juvenile literature. 2. Fiction—Authorship—Juvenile literature. 3. Creative writing—Juvenile literature. I. Title. II. Title: Write a romance in five simple steps.
PN3377.5.L68L54 2012
808.3'85—dc22

2010045044

Future editions:
Paperback ISBN 978-1-4644-0100-8
ePUB ISBN 978-1-4645-1007-6
PDF ISBN 978-1-4646-1007-3

Printed in the United States of America

032012 Lake Book Manufacturing, Inc., Melrose Park, IL

10 9 8 7 6 5 4 3 2 1

To Our Readers: We have done our best to make sure all Internet Addresses in this book were active and appropriate when we went to press. However, the author and the publisher have no control over and assume no liability for the material available on those Internet sites or on other Web sites they may link to. Any comments or suggestions can be sent by e-mail to comments@enslow.com or to the address on the back cover.

Every effort has been made to locate all copyright holders of material used in this book. If any errors or omissions have occurred, corrections will be made in future editions of this book.

Enslow Publishers, Inc., is committed to printing our books on recycled paper. The paper in every book contains 10% to 30% post-consumer waste (PCW). The cover board on the outside of each book contains 100% PCW. Our goal is to do our part to help young people and the environment too!

Cover and Illustration Credits: Shutterstock.com

Contents

Book Key

Keeping a Journal

On the Web

Genre History

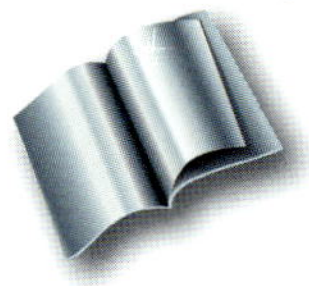

Fun Fact

Check It Out!

Writer's Block

Here's an Idea!

Your Assignment

Organizer

Daydreaming

Step 1

Ideas and Inspiration

If you think you'd like to write a romance novel, start by taking this advice from best-selling romance author Nora Roberts: "Write what you like to read—if you are not captured by the story, who will be?"[1]

It doesn't matter how old you are. If you read romance novels every chance you get, that's probably a good sign that this type of writing is right for you. On the other hand, if you think you'd like to write a romance yet you've never read this type of book, you need to start reading as many romance novels as you can right away.

Authors are busy creating new titles every single day because hungry readers have been known to gobble up as many as forty new romance novels every month. There's room for new authors in this growing market, so now is the perfect time to write your own romance.

Sheri McGregor, author of *Under One Roof,* advises authors to get to know the romance market. "Read in the genre and find where you think your story ideas fit. Get the guidelines. Then write your story with the market in mind, without letting go of your story's heart."[2]

A Few Popular Romance Publishers

You can learn a lot about the romance genre by visiting various publishers' Web sites. Just type the publisher's name into a search engine, for example Google, and check out the site.

Avon Romance - A Division of Harper Collins
Ballantine/Ivy - A Division of Random House
Bantam/Dell - A Division of Random House
Barbour Publishing
Harlequin Publishers

If you go to the Harlequin Publishers Web site, for example, and click on Harlequin Extras, followed by Writing Guidelines, you can see the different lines Harlequin publishes and get the writing guidelines for each line. A line of books is simply a category, subgenre, or type of book. Regency romance would be a specific line that a romance publisher might publish.

When you know exactly what a publisher wants for any line it publishes, it will be much easier to write a story that particular publisher is likely to buy.

Some publishers create imprints for their specific lines. An imprint is like a department of a particular publisher, and books in a specific genre are part of that particular imprint. For example, Silhouette is a Harlequin imprint.

Understanding the Romance Markets

Any type of romance novel should feature a central love story and have an emotionally satisfying ending, of course. However, unlike many other forms of writing, romance is a distinct genre, or category, with many equally distinct subgenres, or subcategories, such as historical romance or paranormal romance.

For this reason, it is a good idea to understand and study examples of these different subgenres before starting to write. The requirements for each subgenre can vary greatly, and they will affect all aspects of your story, the most obvious being the setting and the characters, including their physical appearance, culture, struggles, and actions. The specific subgenre also determines how to write the love scenes and what subjects are taboo.

Finding Inspiration for Your Story

Once you determine the subgenre of romance you'd like to write, you will find inspiration from any number of places.

Many romance authors get their inspiration from real life. Rebecca Winters has written for Harlequin. Winters is a genealogist—someone who studies a family's background and traces their ancestors. Winters says that because she is a genealogist, "I come across amazing stories that take me to different times and continents,"[3] and she is able to use this knowledge of those different times and continents to create her stories.

Romance Subgenres

To help you decide which subgenre is right for you and your story, you'll want to read at least a few novels within each subgenre. Here is a list of the different romance subgenres:

Contemporary Series Romance—These are romance novels released as part of an overall series. The stories in these novels are set after 1945. The main focus of these novels is the romantic relationship of the main characters.

Contemporary Single Title Romance—Each book in this subgenre is released as an individual title, not part of a series. Like contemporary series romance, the focus in these stories is on the romantic relationship, and the stories are set after 1945.

Historical Romance—The stories in these novels can take place in any location and they can be set in any time period before 1945.

Debbie Macomber's romances have sold more than 75 million copies, and she's another writer who draws from real life to create characters and settings for her novels. The picturesque town of Cedar Cove, which is the setting for her Cedar Cove series, was loosely based on her hometown of Port Orchard, Washington, located on the Kitsap Peninsula. Macomber's love of knitting inspired her to create A Good Yarn, a fictional shop on Blossom Street in Seattle for her Blossom Street series.

Inspirational Romance—In this subgenre, religious or spiritual beliefs play a big part in the romantic relationship of the main characters.

Novels With Strong Romantic Elements—In these novels, the romantic relationship between the main characters isn't the major plot, but it is still a big part of the story.

Paranormal Romance—The future, a fantasy world, or other paranormal happenings are a major part of the plot and/or the romance in this subgenre.

Regency Romance—These romance novels are all set against the Regency period of the British Empire.

Romantic Suspense—Suspense, mystery, or thriller elements are important to the plot in this type of romance.

Young Adult Romance—These novels are aimed at young adult readers, so they generally feature younger main characters—in their mid-to-late teens.

Many of Debbie Macomber's characters are knitters, and they go to the fictional store for knitting supplies and knitting classes.

Sometimes real life inspires writers in indirect ways rather than through situations, places, or events that the author has personally experienced. When asked if the main characters for her book *Scarlet Nights* were inspired by any real-life criminals, Jude Deveraux said, "Everything I wrote about Mitzi and Greg is the truth, based on real cases."[4]

Great Romance Fiction

WARNING: Many of these books and films contain mature themes. Ask your parent or guardian for permission before reading or viewing them.

Jane Austen—*Pride and Prejudice*
A story of the lives and loves of five sisters living in England in the early nineteenth century.

Charlotte Brontë—*Jane Eyre*
A young, orphan girl grows into a mature and independent young woman, ultimately winning the heart of the man she loves.

Emily Brontë—*Wuthering Heights*
A tale of a doomed love affair.

Leo Tolstoy—*Anna Karenina*
Chronicles the affairs of a young woman in nineteenth-century Russia.

Gaston Leroux—*The Phantom of the Opera*
A disfigured man hides in a Paris Opera House and terrifies the company's performers.

Edith Wharton—*The Age of Innocence*
A young couple in nineteenth-century New York find their engagement in jeopardy when the man falls for his fiancee's older, scandalized cousin.

Margaret Mitchell—*Gone With the Wind*
An epic romance takes place against the backdrop of the American South during the Civil War and Reconstruction.

Daphne du Maurier—*Rebecca*
A young bride is tortured by constant comparisons to her husband's first wife.

Erich Segal—*Love Story*
A Harvard law student falls for a Radcliffe music student.

Rosamunde Pilcher—*The Shell Seekers*
An older woman finds her memories sparked at the sight of one of her father's paintings and recalls the many secrets and passions of her life.

Julie Garwood—*The Bride*
A Scottish lord is forced to take an English bride.

Jude Deveraux—*A Knight in Shining Armor*
A broken-hearted woman magically finds love four hundred years in the past.

Robert James Waller—*The Bridges of Madison County*
A married but lonely Italian woman living in Iowa in the 1960s finds love with a freelance photographer.

Laura Kinsale—*Flowers From the Storm*
A mute duke is placed in a sanitarium but is saved by the love of a good woman who recognizes his sanity.

Linda Howard—*Dream Man*
A clairvoyant woman witnesses a crime with her strange powers and winds up falling in love with a police detective.

Loretta Chase—*Lord of Scoundrels*
Jessica seeks to protect her brother from the notorious Marquess of Dain, but instead she winds up falling in love with him.

Helen Fielding—*Bridget Jones's Diary*
A British woman decides to keep a diary as she attempts to improve herself and find true love.

Nicholas Sparks—*The Notebook*
A young couple falls in love during the Great Depression; then they are separated by circumstance and have to find their way back to one another.

Gail Carson Levine—*Ella Enchanted*
A retelling of the Cinderella story.

Mary Balogh—*The Temporary Wife*
A marriage of convenience becomes a union of love.

Great Romance Films

***Gone With the Wind* (1939)**
An adaptation of Margaret Mitchell's 1936 novel of the same name.

***Casablanca* (1942)**
A nightclub owner in Casablanca, Morocco, during World War II has to choose between being with the woman he loves or putting the good of the larger world above his own desires.

***Breakfast at Tiffany's* (1961)**
A young man becomes infatuated with a flighty New York socialite that lives in his apartment building.

***Love Story* (1970)**
An adaptation of Erich Segal's 1970 novel of the same name.

***Somewhere in Time* (1980)**
A young man becomes obsessed with the portrait of an actress from decades ago and somehow travels back in time to have an affair with her.

***An Officer and a Gentleman* (1982)**
A loner enters Officer Candidate School to become a navy pilot and also falls in love.

***Ghost* (1990)**
The ghost of a murdered man is pulled back into the world of the living to save the woman he loves.

***Sleepless in Seattle* (1993)**
A young boy tries to play matchmaker for his widowed father by calling in to a radio talk show.

***The English Patient* (1996)**
A young nurse during World War II tries to help a man badly burned in a plane crash to heal from both his injuries and his painful past.

***Romeo and Juliet* (1996)**
An adaptation of Shakespeare's timeless tragedy set in modern times but retaining the Shakespearean language.

***Titanic* (1997)**
An old woman recalls her days as a young socialite, when she fell in love with a poor artist aboard the doomed *HMS Titanic*.

***Ever After: A Cinderella Story* (1998)**
A retelling of the classic story set in France during the Renaissance.

***Notting Hill* (1999)**
A gorgeous movie star falls in love with the owner of a small travel bookstore.

***Bridget Jones's Diary* (2001)**
An adaptation of Helen Fielding's 1996 novel of the same name.

***Pearl Harbor* (2001)**
A love triangle set around the attack on Pearl Harbor.

***A Walk to Remember* (2002)**
A popular bad boy falls for a shy good girl who is keeping a tragic secret.

***Love Actually* (2003)**
Several different romantic stories woven together in modern day London.

***The Notebook* (2004)**
An adaptation of Nicholas Sparks's 1996 novel of the same name.

***Tristan and Isolde* (2006)**
A Cornish knight and an Irish princess fall in love during Europe's Dark Ages.

***The Time Traveler's Wife* (2009)**
A young girl falls in love with a man who can travel through time.

***Crazy Stupid Love* (2011)**
A man tries to get over his cheating wife, while a playboy finds love for the very first time.

***Jane Eyre* (2011)**
An adaptation of Charlotte Brontë's 1847 novel of the same name.

Television has inspired other authors to write romance. Kresley Cole is the #1 *New York Times* best-selling author of the popular Immortals After Dark paranormal series. She got the idea for her book *No Rest for the Wicked* from television. "I was watching The Amazing Race and began thinking: what if the contestants were immortals, the stakes larger than life, and the tasks deadly. The idea grew from there," she says.[5]

Kelly Wallace got the inspiration to write her romance *Lovin' the Cowboy Way* from the movie *Overboard,* starring Goldie Hawn and Kurt Russell. In this movie, Russell plays a single father in need of a wife. Hawn is a spoiled rich woman who falls overboard during a party on a yacht and loses her memory. Russell convinces her she is his wife and his kids' mother. "The movie was hilarious because she had no idea how to take care of kids, cook, or clean due to her pampered upbringing," explains Wallace. "I've always had a love for cowboys and simply created my own version of 'what would happen if . . . ?'"[6]

Another place authors find inspiration is from actual historical events. Yet Cynthia Sterling, who has written several historical romances, cautions authors about this. "I think authors can run into trouble when they plot a romance around specific, big historical events. It's easy to get sidetracked into describing battles or political scandals or other things that take your reader out of the romance."[7] For that reason, she suggests writers use lesser known historical events as inspiration for their novels.

Many romance authors turn to songs for inspiration. When you think about it, songs are just short stories set to music. Romance writers often expand on the stories in songs and turn them into novels.

As a romance writer, you will draw inspiration from all sorts of sources. Even newspapers and other books can give you ideas that can be turned into new novels. Look around. Inspiration and ideas are everywhere!

Writing Exercises

1. Take your laptop or a pad of paper and a pen to your local coffee shop and just hang out. Watch people as they come in and sit down. Pick an interesting-looking couple you see, and make up a short story to tell how they became a couple. Try this same writing exercise at a mall, the park, the supermarket, or the library to see if you come up with different types of couples—some old, some young, some with families, etc.

2. Visit an art museum and choose a painting of an interesting place. Study the painting and turn it into the setting for your next romantic story. What time period will your story take place in this particular setting? Who will your main characters be and how did they come to be in this particular location? Try to create as many details as you can so that anyone who saw this painting would recognize it as the setting for your story.

Step 2

Research

After you've read widely in the subgenre you wish to write for, and you've come up with some ideas for characters, setting, and possible story lines, the next step is to broaden your research.

Now you'll need to make sure you're creating believable characters and settings for the time period in which your story will take place. For example, if you'll be writing a historical novel based on an actual event, you'll need to find out everything you can about this event—and that takes research.

Researching Actual Events

Sandra Brown got the idea for her book *Rainwater* from an incident that her father witnessed during the Depression when he was a child. His father (Brown's grandfather) had a showdown with armed federal agents when they came to his dairy farm and demanded that he pour out milk he couldn't sell because of an over-supplied market. Brown wanted to know more about why this incident had occurred and what was going on at that time with other ranchers and farmers and the government. She conducted extensive research into the various government programs that affected farmers and ranchers at that time. "I used the Internet for newspaper stories and tapped into various libraries to read journals and printed transcripts of interviews."[1]

Learning About Customs, Manners, and Language of Other Times

Robin Schone had to do extensive research for her book *Awaken, My Love,* which takes place during the Victorian era. She often researches little details to get them right. "If writing a scene where, say, my hero plunges his hands into his pockets, I quick check to make sure that trousers in that era did indeed possess pockets."[2]

A good way to find out about all the little details of Regency life is by combing through personal diaries, journals, and letters of actual people who lived during that period. Some of these materials can be found online. They will really bring history to life and give you more ideas for creating a great story your readers will love.

After awhile you probably won't need to do such extensive research each time you write a new Regency romance because you'll already be an expert on this era, just like Regency author Tracy Anne Warren. She says, "The Regency period in England is a very familiar one for me after years of study on the subject, so most of my research is done on an as needed basis during the writing of my books."[3]

Where and How to Research

Most writers today, whether they write fiction or nonfiction, do a great deal (if not all) of their research online. However, you may choose other sources for your research, too. If you live in a town with a large university, pay a visit to its library. You won't be able to borrow items from the library if you are not a student there. But you might be able to make use of its collection of books, magazines, and other periodicals while you're there.

University libraries sometimes have a more extensive collection of old magazines than small, local, public libraries have. But there is always the potential for discovery, even in a smaller library. You might be pleasantly surprised at all you find there, particularly if you ask the librarian to help you with your research. For the most part, librarians love research, so don't be afraid to ask for assistance. They may be able to point you to a resource you never would have thought of using otherwise.

Local Historical Societies

Does your story take place in your hometown years ago (before you were even born, perhaps)? Older relatives and friends can be good resources for learning about the past. Still, you should not rely solely upon people you know for information about what your town was like in "the good old days."

One of the best potential sources of information about local history is a local historical society, if there is one close to where you live. Most historical societies have genealogy files, files on topics of local interest, old maps, newspaper almanacs, original photographs and documents, artifacts, and directories that will really help you bring history to life in your story. They will also let you know about the national and state historic sites in your area that you can visit so you can get a real feel for how people lived when the sites were first constructed.

Tourist and Convention Centers

If you want to write a contempory romance set in a city you aren't familiar with, the local tourist or convention center for that town or city is a great place to get information. While you will create fictional businesses and homes in your story, you still might want to include references to real local monuments and other actual points of interest that many readers will recognize. This will help you get the reader more involved in the tale you're telling.

Museums

Most cities have local museums of one sort or another. Museums are excellent places to see examples of clothing, household, and personal items from a specific time and place. But you'll need to find a museum that contains the type of materials specific to the time and place you'll be writing about. Fortunately, most major museums also have Web sites with access to many helpful documents, photos, and other materials online.

Local Professionals

Local professionals can also be great sources of information for authors. For her book *Scarlet Nights,* Jude Deveraux went to her friend Detective Charlie Stack for help. "He directed me to books and websites and he answered all my questions, whether I asked about martial arts or economic crimes."[4] Depending on your story, you could interview a local police officer, doctor, dance instructor, or other professionals. They may be more than happy to help you. It doesn't hurt to try.

No matter what kind of information you need to know in order to bring your characters and your story to life, there is a way to find that information. And, who knows, you just might discover that research is something you really love.

Writing Exercises

1. Visit one of the Web sites listed in the addendum to research a particular time period in British history. Use the information you get to create a heroine for your story. Describe her—her clothes, her hairstyle, her mannerisms. Try to write a few lines of dialogue for her that are appropriate for the time and place in which she lived.

2. Google "fashions during World War II" to find various Web sites that will give you more information about the kinds of clothes people wore during this time in history. Use this information to develop a heroine for a story. Describe her clothing in great detail. As you learn why people wore the types of clothing they did at this time, use this information to help build your heroine's character and background.

Step 3

Organization

All writers work a little differently. Some writers do extensive research and use a variety of tools to help gather and organize the information they will need to have before they can start writing.

Other writers are so prolific, they don't seem to need time for research or organization. Barbara Cartland was known as the "Queen of Romance" because she managed to write more than seven hundred romance novels during seven decades. For many years, she completed a new romance novel every fourteen days! However, according to the BBC News in a report of Cartland's death on May 21, 2000, Cartland didn't actually write all those novels. "Dressed in pink chiffon and adorned with enormous false eyelashes, she dictated her stories to a secretary."[1]

You probably won't dress in pink chiffon and dictate your stories to a secretary, the way Barbara Cartland did. You probably won't turn out a new romance novel every fourteen days either. But you will want to use at least a few of the tools most published writers rely on to collect and organize their information before they start writing.

An Idea Notebook

As you start writing your romance, you're bound to get new ideas for characters, plot lines, locations to include in the story, etc. No doubt, some of the best ideas will come to you when you aren't sitting at your computer or writing desk, so it's a good idea to get a pocket-size notebook you can keep with you at all times. Use it to jot down all your great, and even those not-so-great, ideas.

A Project Folder

You also might want to create a project folder. This is just a large manila file folder where you'll keep notes, pictures you tear out of magazines, your notecards with research info—just anything that pertains to the novel you are working on.

A Vision Board

Some writers find that it helps them to write about their characters and the settings if they can actually "see" these story elements. To do that, they comb through magazines looking for pictures of people and places that look somewhat like the people and places they envision for their story. All these photos can be stored in the project folder until it's time to start writing. Then the photos can be tacked up on a bulletin board above your computer or writing desk to create a vision board for your novel. As you're introducing the heroine, for example, look closely at the magazine picture you've chosen to represent her. Describe the details you see in this picture so your readers will be able to "see" your heroine as clearly as you do.

Story Maps

A good way to keep all the facts straight when you set your story in a fictional town is to make a map of your town. Figure out the various locations within this town that will be mentioned in your book, then map out where each of these spots is located. That way, you'll remember where each landmark, restaurant, and other spot mentioned in your story is supposed to be. You'll also begin to really "feel" as if the town you're creating is a real place, making it easier to bring that place to life for your readers.

Jude Deveraux says, "I have to have floor plans for wherever the people are, whether it's a mansion, an apartment, or a ship. When they go out the door, I need to know which way they need to turn to get out."[2] A story map can help writers keep track of these kinds of little details.

Character Profiles and Interviews

Before you figure out what your story line or plot will be, you need to get to know your characters. A character profile is just a list of basic information about a character in your story. It gives you a way to get to know some basic information

you will need to be persistent and patient. While you are looking, you can also take the opportunity to go back and look over your work. You might have an idea to improve your story—and the better your story is, the better chance you have at landing an agent or publisher. Once again, it is a good idea to join the Romance Writers of America (RWA). This is a well-respected organization where you'll meet other romance writers and learn all the nuts and bolts of writing and publishing romance. Once you get to know a few published authors in the group, you can ask them about their experiences with agents and publishers. You can also join Internet discussion lists for romance writers and frequently visit various romance authors' Web sites where they will sometimes give information and advice about agents.

"Get a copy of *Writer's Market*," suggests author Karen Kingsbury. "This is an informational book that releases new every year and has a list of editors and agents who are acquiring new material."[1] *The Guide to Literary Agents* by Writers Digest Books is also a helpful tool. It gives detailed information on many agents regarding the type of work they wish to represent, what they want to see from authors, etc.

If You Choose to Self-Publish

If you decide to publish your novel yourself, one of the easiest ways to do that is to go with a publisher who offers print-on-demand (called POD) services. Print on demand just means books are printed as you need them. Most print-on-demand publishers offer an entire publishing package, which includes everything from having the cover created for your book, getting the ISBN number and Library of Congress Number for your book, printing the book, then mailing it out to anyone who buys it.

But there are many ways to self-publish your romance. Lisa Shea says, "I have self published three books on medieval romance in order to test various self-publishing options."[2] On her Web site, she offers tips and step-by step guides to self-publishing.

Before you make a decision about how your book will be published, learn all you can about traditional publishing and self-publishing. There are pros and cons to each method.

Writing Exercises

1. Now that you're about to become a published author, you'll need a short author biography for the back cover of your book. You should write this biography in third person, and it should simply be two to three sentences about you. Read the author biographies on the back covers of some of your favorite romance novels for examples.

2. Pretend your first romance novel has been a huge hit, and now your editor has suggested you turn this book into a series. Start thinking of how this same cast of characters (at least your hero and your heroine) can be featured in at least two more books!

Chapter Notes

Step 1: Ideas and Inspiration

1. “An Interview With Nora Roberts,” *Book Browse Page,* n.d., <http://www.bookbrowse.com/author_interviews/full/index.cfm?author_number=296> (July 12, 2010).

2. “How to Write a Romance Novel,” *eHow,* n.d., <http://www.ehow.com/how_16733_write-romance-novel.html> (August 6, 2010).

3. “Rebecca Winters” *Harlequin Romance Authors,* n.d., <http://www.harlequinromanceauthors.com/authors/meet_winters.html> (August 23, 2010).

4.“Interview With Jude Deveraux,” *Simon & Schuster Author’s Page,* n.d., <http://authors.simonandschuster.com/Jude Deveraux/1445134/interview> (June 6, 2010).

5. “Kresley Cole, Author Revealed, Simon & Schuster,” *Simon & Schuster Author Page,* n.d., <http://authors.simonandschuster.com/KresleyCole/19974464/author_revealed> (August 23, 2010).

6. Cherokee, “An Interview With Kelly Wallace,” *Coffeetime Romance,* n.d., <http://coffeetimeromance.com/Interviews/KellyWallace.html> (July 6, 2010).

7. Cynthia Sterling, “A Quickie on Historical Accuracy,” *All About Romance,* n.d., <http://www.likesbooks.com/quick15.html> (July 8, 2010).

Step 2: Research

1. "Interview With Sandra Brown," *Simon & Schuster Author Page,* n.d., <http://authors.simonandschuster.com/SandraBrown/19338053/interview> (June 6, 2010).
2. "ARR Interview With Robin Schone," *A Romantic Review Page,* n.d., <http://www.aromancereview.com/interviews/robinschone.phtml> (August 2, 2010).
3. Debbie (no surname), "ARR Interview With Tracy Anne Warren," *A Romantic Review Page,* n.d., <http://www.aromancereview.com/interviews/tracyannewarren.phtml> (August 2, 2010).
4. "Interview With Jude Deveraux," *Simon & Schuster Author's Page,* n.d., <http://authors.simonandschuster.com/JudeDeveraux/1445134/interview> (June 6, 2010).

Step 3. Organization

1. "Barbara Carland Dies," *BBC News,* May 21, 2000, <http://news.bbc.co.uk/2/hi/uk_news/758077.stm> (August 27, 2010).
2. "Interview With Jude Deveraux," *Simon & Schuster Author's Page,* n.d., <http://authors.simonandschuster.com/JudeDeveraux/1445134/interview> (June 6, 2010).

Step 4. Writing

1. "An Interview With Nora Roberts," B*ook Browse Page,* n.d., <http://www.bookbrowse.com/author_interviews/full/index.cfm?author_number=296> (July 12, 2010).
2. Debbie (no surname), "Interview With Laura Lee Guhrke," *A Romantic Review News,* n.d., <http://www.aromancereview.com/interviews/lauraleeguhrke.phtml> (August 5, 2010).

3. Dawn Arkin, "Romance Writing 101," *Romance Fiction Factor Page,* n.d., <http://romance.fictionfactor.com/articles/romance101.html> (May 3, 2010).

Step 5. Publish

1. Karen Kingsbury, "Ten Tips for Aspiring Authors," *Karen Kingsbury,* n.d., <http://karenkingsbury.com/writingTips/> (August 10, 2010).

2. Lea Shea, "Getting Your Book Published," *Lisa Shea .com,* n.d., <http://www.lisashea.com/lisabase/writing/gettingyourbookpublished/index.html> (August 28, 2010).

Glossary

Cinderella stories—Stories where the poor, unattractive heroine is suddenly transformed and attracts the attention of the handsome hero.

close/forced proximity—The two main characters are forced to spend time together in tight quarters and a romance develops between them.

conflict—The events or situations that drive the plot in a romance or other novel or story. Typically, the main characters must overcome both internal and external conflicts. These conflicts create rising action that leads to a climax (the most exciting part of the novel) before the conflicts are all solved or resolved.

friends-to-lovers stories—The hero and heroine start out as friends but later discover they have much deeper feelings for each other.

hero/heroine—In a romance novel, the two major characters (protagonists). Typically, during the course of the novel, the hero and heroine will meet, resist each other at the beginning of the story, but eventually fall in love.

narrative hook—A technique used by an author to "hook" the reader's attention at the very start of the story so he/she will continue reading.

plot—The series of events that make up the story of a novel or short story.

point of view (POV)—The perspective from which the story is told. Most romance novels are told from a first-person ("I") POV or a third-person ("He" or "she") POV.

setting—The time, location, and circumstances in which the story takes place.

wholesome romance—A romance novel with a sweet story line and no explicit love scenes.

Further Reading

Books

Benke, Karen. *Rip the Page!: Adventures in Creative Writing*. Boston, Mass.: Roost Books, 2010.

Elish, Dan. *The Craft of Writing: Fiction*. Salt Lake City, Utah: Benchmark Books, 2011.

Farrell, Tish. *Be a Creative Writer*. Tunbridge Wells: TickTock, 2010.

Hanley, Victoria. *Seize the Story*. Austin, Tex.: Prufrock Press, Inc., 2011.

Mazer, Anne, and Ellen Potter. *Spilling Ink: A Young Writer's Handbook*. New York: Roaring Brook Press, 2010.

Strausser, Jeffrey. *Painless Writing*. 2nd edition. New York: Barron's, 2009.

Sutherland, Joel A. *Be a Writing Superstar*. Markham, Ontario: Scholastic Canada, 2010.

Internet Addresses

Nicholas Sparks: The Official Website
http://www.nicholassparks.com/

JaneAusten.org
http://www.janeausten.org/

Kids on the Net: Creative Writing
http://www.kidsonthenet.org.uk/create/index.cfm

The Craft of Writing Fiction
http://www.craftingfiction.com/

The Passionate Pen: Romance Publishers
http://www.passionatepen.com/romancepubs.htm

TeenInk
http://www.teenink.com/

Romance Writers of America
http://www.rwanational.org/

Addendum

Resource Sites

Here are a few helpful resource sites for those interested in writing historical romances.

ANCIENT EGYPT

The British Museum: Ancient Egypt

http://www.ancientegypt.co.uk/menu.html

The British Museum's site detailing ancient Egyptian life, geography, religion, and the role of the pharaoh.

KingTutOne.com

http://www.kingtutone.com/

Information on the famous "boy pharaoh" King Tut, the pyramids, mummies, rulers, and the Ancient Egyptian belief system.

MIDDLE AGES

Middle Ages: Medieval Sources

http://www.themiddleages.net/

Includes a list of famous people of the Middle Ages, information on the bubonic plague, and descriptions of medieval dances, lifestyles, entertainment, weapons, and more.

Middle Ages

http://www.middle-ages.org.uk/

Information on many aspects of medieval life, including clothing, society, government, food, and warfare.

COLONIAL AMERICA

Passport to Colonial Times

http://eev.liu.edu/kk/colonial/resources.htm

Information on food, clothes, occupations, and what life was like for women and children.

Colonial America

http://www.us-roots.org/colonialamerica/index.html

Includes census records and information about each of the original colonies, important conflicts, colonial government, and daily life.

AMERICAN OLD WEST

The Wild West

http://www.thewildwest.org/

Includes American Indian and cowboy facts.

NativeTech: Native American Technology and Art

http://www.nativetech.org/

Contains articles on clothing, pottery, toys, food, and more.

REGENCY PERIOD

Austentation: Regency Accessories

http://www.austentation.com/

Describes the accessories worn during the Regency period, including cosmetics, jewelry, hats, undergarments, and shoes.

Jane Austen's World: Social Customs During the Regency Era

http://janeaustensworld.wordpress.com/social-customs-and-the-regency-world/

Contains an extensive list of sources on such things as food, fashion, currency, music, weddings, funerals, vocabulary, and much more.

MISCELLANEOUS

Ellis Island

http://www.ellisisland.org/

Has a search engine for finding passengers who entered the United States through Ellis Island.

Ivan Day's Historic Food Site

http://www.historicfood.com/portal.htm

A site on European culinary history including recipes, recreations of meals and table décor, and food molds.

Self-Publishing Options

Here are some of the most well-known and reputable publishers who offer print-on-demand services.

Xlibris
http://www2.xlibris.com/

BookLocker
http://www.booklocker.com

CreateSpace
http://www.createspace.com

LuLu
http://www.lulu.com

E-Book Publishers

An e-publisher is a great place to start submitting your work. The turnaround time at many e-publishers is usually quicker than with print publishers, and new authors are discovered by e-publishers all the time.

Awe-Struck Press
http://www.awe-struck.net/index.html

The Wild Rose Press
http://www.thewildrosepress.com

Uncial Press
http://www.uncialpress.com/

Index